EVIDENCE-BASED
HORSE
MANSHIP

DR. STEPHEN PETERS & MARTIN BLACK

Wasteland Press

www.wastelandpress.net
Shelbyville, KY USA

Evidence-Based Horsemanship
by Dr. Stephen Peters & Martin Black

Second Printing – May 2023
Paperback ISBN: 978-1-60047-685-3
Hardback ISBN: 978-1-68111-402-6
eBook available via Kindle, Nook, and Apple Books

Photography by Kim Stone. Stone's images have appeared in numerous books and publications. Her photography can be seen at www.shinanatu.com

Additional photographic contributions were made by Peters, Jennifer Black (including black mare and bottle), Joyce Peters (science photography), Adam Pennarola, and Maddy Butcher.
Photo of Randy Rieman by Ross Hecox, Western Horseman
Photo on page xii of Martin Black by Kate Bradley, Western Horseman.

Front and back cover photo and design by Maddy Butcher

Printed in the U.S.A.

0   1   2   3   4   5   6   7   8   9   10   11   12   13

FOREWORD

For thousands of years, horses and humans have had a partnership both remarkable and unique in the animal kingdom. We have combined our strengths by uniting our minds, bodies, and wills to accomplish tasks together. These tasks have ranged from mundane and routine to epic and heroic with outcomes ranging from tragic to triumphant.

It was horsepower on the hoof, not under the hood, that shaped our early life here in the West. With horses, we multiplied our strength, improved our mobility, expanded our territory, plowed our fields, planted our seeds, harvested our crops, hauled our freight, skidded our timber, powered our mills, transported our troops, and handled our cattle.

In those bygone days, the horse was an intimate part of daily life and a large percentage of our population had a basic working knowledge of horses – a.k.a. horsemanship.

Enter the industrial age, mechanization, and a mass exodus from rural America to urban America. That common knowledge quickly became uncommon as horsemanship skills disappeared from the general public.

For the last 100 years, Amish farms and western ranches have been about the only places where horses remained an integral part of daily life. It is on the western ranches in particular where good horsemanship continued to be held in high esteem.

Fast-forward to the year 2012 and we find ourselves living in a virtual wonderland of the greatest technological advancements and devices in history. Space travel is common. High speed messaging is routine. Personal computers, Internet, cell phones, global access, MRI chambers, CAT scan machines -- full 3D imaging of the entire human body inside and out. Incredible!

Oddly enough, in the midst of this tornado of technology, we are also living in a time of renaissance, a renaissance of horsemanship. What was old is new again.

The word renaissance is defined: 1. A rebirth or revival 2. A revival of intellectual or artistic achievement.

Now, if you don't think horsemanship qualifies as both an intellectual AND artistic achievement, then you've not seen fine horsemanship. This renaissance of horsemanship has been occurring here in the United States for about three decades, smack dab in the middle of the information age. It's no accident. This new interest in good horsemanship owes much to the technological advancements that make information so easily accessible today.

So, here we are in the middle of a rebirth of interest in horsemanship AND a golden age of information exchange. What a perfect time for a scientist, Dr. Stephen Peters, and a horseman, Mr. Martin Black, to combine their considerable knowledge and expertise concerning horses. That is just what they've done in *Evidence-Based Horsemanship*.

Most horsemen agree you need accurate information and years of experience and experimentation to turn that information into knowledge. They also agree that timing, feel, and balance are the holy trinity of horsemanship. These are also the key ingredients for success in many other areas of life.

As for this new book, the "timing" couldn't be better. We are in the midst of a revival of interest in horsemanship. People are hungry for factual information, intelligent conversation, and astute observation about how horses learn, think, react, and respond. The book is filled with that information.

The "feel" of the book is genuinely refreshing and original, introducing factual information few have been privy to. It is unpretentious, straight forward, and informative.

The "balance" of the book is brilliant. It is a combination of scientific facts and the empirical evidence to support those facts assembled by two highly respected professionals in their respective disciplines.

Dr. Stephen Peters is a scientist and neuropsychologist with decades of experience and a deep understanding of the processes of brain function, neurochemistry, and how they impact the learning process.

Martin Black is a horseman and clinician with decades of experience and a deep understanding of the subtleties of animal behavior and the modification of that behavior.

Together, in *Evidence-Based Horsemanship*, these men are exploring and bringing to light some of the mysteries of successfully interacting with horses.

Bill Dorrance once confessed this statement to me: "I found out that if I wasn't learning, life got kinda dull."

I have a notion he would be excited about this book because it sure presents an opportunity to learn!

Dr. Peters and Mr. Black have done more than swing the bat. They've hit a home run with *Evidence-Based Horsemanship*.

-Randy Rieman

INTRODUCTIONS

Dr. Stephen Peters

In an effort to determine and apply 'best practices,' evidence-based approaches are common in medicine. Best practices are determined by empirical evidence. They are seen to work or not work in actual practice, not theory.

These clinical observations are supported by the most current scientific knowledge and allow for a standard approach to decision-making and problem-solving. Medical insurance companies now demand evidence-based approaches because they are only willing to pay for what has been shown to work. This approach bridges the gap between the scientist and the clinical practitioner.

What application could this possibly have for horsemanship?

Scientific technology has produced sophisticated equipment that allows us to ask questions we had no way of asking in the past. For example, functional MRI (fMRI, a brain imaging method) now allows us to identify which specific brain regions are being used in real time as a person is performing a cognitive task (e.g., responding to questions, looking at pictures, performing motor tasks).

Recently, researchers who allowed subjects to rest in the fMRI between tasks found that the same brain areas used in performing the task were still being used by the subjects while resting. When retested, those subjects also seemed to incorporate the knowledge from that task better than subjects who were not exposed to a delay. Might this also be what is occurring in the horse when given time to "dwell?"

Over time, we've seen a large amount of more sophisticated data on horses. People are hungry for information. With the use of the Internet, they are able to locate immediate sources of knowledge. I think these trends will eventually lead us to a more evidence-based approach with horses.

However, there still appears to be a large information gap between available knowledge and what is practiced in the horse world. Many decisions seem to be based on information of variable quality, supposed expert opinion, tradition, or trial and error. Often opinions are diametrically opposed, leaving the inquirer with five different opinions from five different experts. Statements such as, "I've been doing this for 50 years" doesn't negate the fact that someone can do something wrong for 50 years.

An Evidence-Based Horsemanship (EBH) approach would be based on outcomes and rely on observations informed by the most current scientific knowledge. Egos, persuasive salespeople, and charismatic personalities would have little relevance to EBH.

EBH would help disprove myths as well as help confirm and validate the empirical findings of people with deep understanding and expertise. They may have observed and interpreted the subtlest signals from a horse, but lacked a language to communicate their findings.

By profession, I am a neuropsychologist and specialize in brain functioning. In training my own horses, I wanted a better understanding of the neurofunctioning of the horse's brain. I also became quite frustrated by hearing such things as, "the horse has two brains," or "the horse is trying to make a chump of me," or using a pop psychology test designed to arrive at a personality type for your horse.

In actuality, the horse has one brain with two hemispheres well-connected by a structure called the corpus callosum. The horse brain is about the size of a large grapefruit and is proportionately 1/650th of their body weight (The human brain is 1/50th of our body weight.) They have a large cerebellum for balance and smooth movement. Most of the brain area is dedicated to motor and sensory functions.

Horses do not have a huge frontal lobe like humans, so they are unable to make fun of someone and return to share the joke with their pasture mates. Although they have personalities based on how they behave, it would be anthropomorphic to assign human personality traits to these animals. The temptation to want to believe horses process things in the same way as humans may make us feel better but it is inaccurate, leads to false assumptions, and is often at the expense of the horse's welfare and well-being.

This collaboration grew out of a meeting with Martin Black while attending the Legacy of Legends clinic in honor of the late Ray Hunt and Tom Dorrance. I had placed Ray Hunt and especially Tom Dorrance in the category of experts with special powers of observation when it came to reading the subtleties involved in human-horse interaction and communication. Martin Black, a fifth-generation cowboy, is a well-known horseman and clinician who worked with and was influenced by Hunt and Dorrance.

I decided to write a book about horses' neurofunctioning and brain-behavior relationships. I wanted to compare my research findings with the experiences of someone with a wealth of empirical information. I especially wanted to speak with Martin, who has observed horses for decades. He is also known for working with riders and starting hundreds of colts each year.

Little did I know our discussion would turn into more meetings, numerous e-mails, and a collaboration. I found Martin himself to be a good scientist: focused on his subject instead of himself, possessing an insatiable desire to learn, and basing his opinions on objective observation of thousands of horses.

Observations that Martin had made for years, I could corroborate with evidence based on the horses' central nervous system, autonomic nervous system, and neurochemistry. Putting these pieces of the puzzle together, empirical observation informed by science, is the essence of Evidence-Based Horsemanship.

We both feel that this information could be the tip of the iceberg in developing "best practices" with a common language that everyone can understand and apply. EBH is an approach that continually evolves as our knowledge base grows. Finding that one has done something the wrong way may be just as valuable as getting it right, if it refines the knowledge base so others do not have to struggle with a similar wrong turn.

This approach is not concerned with arguing over a school of thought or following one trainer over another. There is room for everyone under this umbrella to educate themselves by asking, "What does our current scientific knowledge of the horse, when applied and empirically observed, show me about getting the best outcomes possible for me and the horse? Does it work? What's the proof? What is it based on?"

Eventually, people should be able to obtain current best practices in all areas of horse care. Finally and best of all, a deeper understanding from quality information will be what is best for the welfare of our horses. I think Tom and Ray would be okay with that.

Martin Black

When I was young working cattle there was a noticeable difference in how cattle responded if you worked them slow and quiet versus getting fast with them and getting them scared. When they were slow and had time to think they would usually make choices that were more helpful to us and there was a point when you would get fast that this helpfulness would shut down and they would only try to protect themselves.

At the time, I was only riding older, more seasoned horses and didn't consider this observation with cattle and how it would relate to horses. As I got older and started riding colts it became obvious that most of the trouble I would have would be when the horse felt like it needed to protect itself. At the time I did not realize what made it happen but I did realize that there was a difference.

Later when I got around Tom Dorrance, I could see he was very keen at recognizing the difference and calculating how he would use the comfort or self-preservation to motivate the horse. As I worked with more horses I learned that when we are passive we get a certain response from the horse and when we are aggressive we get a different response from the horse. When we are too passive, horses may get bored and lose interest with us and if we are too aggressive they can get too protective. But when we get the balance just right the horse can operate at a place where he is interested but not worried. The more they can experience operating at this place, the more they look for this place because it feels good to them.

Although I had a sense that there may be some chemical reaction inside the animals, it wasn't until I met Steve and he explained how the neurochemical system works that it really made sense to me. After learning more of his knowledge it really helped me to understand in more depth what I have experienced and witnessed Tom doing.

My experience on ranches working around people who use alcohol and drugs, and seeing how certain drugs or chemicals can make people happy, sad, sleepy, lovable, or want to fight, made me think there was some relation in the attitude of horses. I knew a little bit about adrenaline and dopamine, but there's a lot I didn't know or understand and didn't give it enough consideration. After working with Steve and trading information with him, he has helped me fill in some gray areas and I feel I have a much more complete understanding of the horse.

When we can and cannot compare human brains to horse brains:

Brain cells, brain molecules, neurotransmitters and synapses are almost identical in ALL animals. At this level, animals are made from the same essential building blocks.

When discussing brain function, it's helpful to first consider the human brain, the most developed of all animals.

We can think of it as having three progressive layers or even three brains. The layers have distinct functions but their interactions are essential and considerable.

The reptilian brain (consisting of the brain stem and cerebellum) is concerned with survival and body maintenance. Digestion, reproduction, circulation, breathing, and the 'flight or fight' response are all reptilian brain functions.

The second layer is the limbic system. It includes the amygdala and hippocampus and involves emotion and memory. The limbic system concerns itself with primitive activities related to food, sex, and bonding. It is responsible for memories of behaviors connected to agreeable and disagreeable experiences. In humans, we call them emotions.

The third layer is the neocortex or cerebral cortex. It is the largest part of the human brain. Language, speech, and writing are all possible because of this layer.

We can think of the horse brain as having stopped its development just short of this massive thinking lobe. Nonetheless, horses and humans have the two first brain layers in common. So we can compare research and data of horse and human brain functioning at this level. But the higher functioning areas of the brain do not exist in horses and it would be wrong to compare brains at this level.

A note about the text:

To clarify the speaker, Martin Black's comments appear in boxes. All other commentary may be attributed to Dr. Steve Peters.

Also, Dr. Peters uses purposeful repetition of terms, concepts, and words throughout the text in order to give the reader greater familiarity with the complicated nature of neurology.

A note about the glossary:

To help readers, we have developed a glossary at the back of this book. Words defined in the glossary are often marked in bold when first mentioned.

EVIDENCE—BASED
HORSE
MANSHIP

CHAPTER ONE

MYELINATION and DEVELOPMENT

The horse is born much more "ready for life" than humans. If the horse is going to survive, nature must equip it with the ability to stand up quickly and move. It is the process of **myelination** that contributes to this rapid brain growth and maturation.

Myelin is a fatty substance that works like an insulator covering nerve fibers which transmit information. These fibers are laid down in extensive pathways throughout the brain.

These pathways are like millions of small wires carrying electrochemical messages. These tracks are insulated by the fatty myelin that gives them a white appearance. The heavily myelinated areas are often referred to as white matter.

The myelin insulation on these nerve fibers allows information to travel at an extremely high rate of speed compared to non-insulated fibers. A car can certainly travel faster down a newly paved highway than an old back road filled with potholes. One could think of myelin as the highway pavement. In this case, it's an information highway.

In the foal, myelin grows rapidly during the first 40 to 50 days. As you will discover in the course of reading this book, the horse's brain is much more a motor and sensory organ than it is a thinking one.

Because the motor and locomotion pathways are the most critical to the foal's survival, these are the first to become fully myelinated. We are paving this highway first so

1

the horse can move in a coordinated fashion, stick with its mother, and move with a herd.

Brain development and alterations in the density of white matter can be influenced by the electrical activity of the nerve fibers themselves. In other words, as the horse moves, it sends signals along the motor tracks influencing the myelination. The foal will stretch and move in various positions quite a bit, thereby stimulating these motor messages.

From the very first day of life, energetic stretching occurs. Researchers have estimated that close to 100 stretches per day can be seen by the third day of life. The stretching behavior strengthens these motor pathways and signals and enables rapid myelination to take place.

During the first six weeks, foals will attempt to eat their mother's manure. This behavior, called corprophagia, is common and important. It helps the foal to obtain intestinal microbes and bacteria needed for digestive functioning in its new environment. Perhaps more importantly, it helps the foal acquire a special chemical called deoxycholic acid. Deoxycholic acid plays a key role in supporting proper myelination.

Horses neurodevelopment reflects the progressive pathway of myelination:

motor roots –>> sensory roots –>> brainstem auditory and vestibular tracks –>> cerebellum –>> optic nerve –>> corticospinal tract –>> optic/acoustic radiations –>> Association cortex.

The development of myelin starts with motor roots because movement is the top priority. Following the myelination of motor roots come the tracks for sensations. The brainstem pathways (involving many automatic behaviors and where the spinal cord meets the brain) continue to develop. Motor patterns of this immature brain are mostly under the brainstem's control.

At this point, no real thinking is involved. The tracks and myelination to the more advanced brain center connections have not yet been developed.

The next key area of connection is to the cerebellum (One of the most important structures in the horse's brain and one we will look at in depth later on). The myelination of this pathway allows the cerebellum to coordinate and smooth out the horse's movement. The reason for such herky-jerky movement in foals is because the cerebellum and its connections are not fully developed.

The cerebellum will also play a role in controlling balance, head, and eye movements. For the rest of the horse's life, the cerebellum will act as a library for storing all learning regarding physical movement.

The optic nerve and its connections to visual areas of the brain will be laid down along with more extensive paths from the spine to the brain. The horse's brain at this stage is plastic or malleable. Up to age four and into adulthood, new interconnections will continue to be myelinated through the brain.

During gestation, the fetus' brain matures and develops. This maturation eventually results in a smooth flow of nerve signals throughout the brain and also makes connections with all the different brain areas.

Brain signals are sent electrochemically. The chemicals involved in signals are called neurotransmitters or neurochemicals. Electrical activity of axons (large groupings of nerve fibers) will influence myelination.

From a neurochemical standpoint, we now know that learning begets more learning. The release of a neurochemical called **glutamate** (the major excitatory neurotransmitter) influences myelination. Glutamate stimulates communication between large groups of nerve fibers and **glial cells**. Glial cells are the glue that binds and connects nerve fibers through growth.

In the developing brain of a young horse, repeated sequences of motor movements will facilitate myelination.

In other words, the horse's behavior can influence the development of axons or nerve fibers. This concept is supported by studies showing that training creates changes in white matter architecture. In humans, one study showed extensive piano practicing in children created more white matter tracts in regions of the brain related to piano playing.

Myelination develops and advances first in the brain areas most necessary for the horse's survival. Primitive frontal lobe connections are the last to be wired. As we will discuss later, the primitive frontal lobe is involved in attention and movement initiation.

From foal to age two, the horse has a limited attention span, comparable to that of a young child. From age two to four, its attention span is like a human teenager's.

Putting these horses to work in long training sessions would be equivalent to asking a third grader to attend and take notes at a lengthy college lecture. Instead, short and simple training sessions are most effective at this age.

The CEREBELLUM and MEMORY for SKILLS, HABITS, and CONDITIONING:

The **cerebellum** acts to integrate sensorimotor information to produce smooth, coordinated movement. The **flocculonodular lobe** of the cerebellum also processes information and controls coordinated movements of the head and eye.

Head posture and coordination are controlled by the cerebellar and vestibular regions in response to sensory input from the head, limbs and trunk. Smooth coordination of head movements are controlled by the cerebellum. Axons from the vestibular nuclei project to the cerebellum.

The cerebellum directly registers the sensation of pressure on the horse's limbs and body, dictating natural reaction to pressure while coordinating voluntary movement. This system is responsible for the learning and storage of physical movements:

Motor routines run through the cerebellum –>> basal ganglia –>> primitive frontal lobe (motor learning).

The horse's brain is wired for movement routines.

Learned motor skills and perceptual motor skills are embedded in procedures and can be expressed through performance. We can learn a motor skill without having any awareness at all of what is being learned. In imaging studies, investigators have found that several areas of brain are specifically activated during sequence learning. These areas include the sensorimotor cortex, the **caudate nucleus** and

putamen, deep brain structures known to be involved in motor learning. Functional MRI has also shown that practice recruits activity of additional neurons in the motor cortex.

Motor skill learning probably occurs in changes within the circuits already dedicated to performing the skill in question. An interesting feature of motor skill learning is that there is a shift in which specific brain systems are important. This experience suggests areas of the brain involved in attention and awareness may be needed early in skill training but these areas become less important as learning proceeds.

The cerebellum is important during the earlier stages of motor skill learning. It is necessary for coordinating the specific repertoire of movements that are needed for well-executed, skilled motion and for organizing the timing of these movements. The cerebellum ensures that the correct movements are assembled together. With the caudate nucleus and putamen, the cerebellum stores skill-based information in long-term memory.

To learn a motor skill is to acquire a procedure for operating in the world. The hippocampus, what we typically consider a memory and learning center is <u>not</u> required in remembering information gradually acquired through repetition.

Horses learn by habit. They gradually discriminate – to scratch against the best tree, to roll on the best surface, to drink from the best water spot. Learning proceeds gradually as the horse learns the relevant dimensions of the problem. They sense any changes in conditions and surroundings.

They can learn gradually without depending on the hippocampus because they are not memorizing but slowly mastering the problem as we would a skill like hitting a ball with a bat.

The ability to predict positive feedback, i.e., dopamine release, is central to the learning process. The caudate nucleus contains a high percentage of neurons that use dopamine as a neurotransmitter. Dopamine neurons in the neostriatum (including the caudate and putamen) are likely to be an important internal mechanism for reward-driven and feedback-driven learning.

The caudate and putamen receive overlapping inputs from the sensory cortex and motor cortex. This double set of inputs could form a basis for associating stimuli and responses. One possibility is that habit learning occurs when dopamine release produces synaptic changes in cortical nerves that are active just before the reward was presented.

We would like to think that dopamine is only released when the horse learns something positive, but it isn't necessarily so. Consider potentially stressful situations such as trailer loading:

The horse may load into a trailer and find a release of pressure as the trailer is closed up and he finds hay to eat. There may be a dopamine release and a learning moment here.

Alternatively, the horse may pull back, get away from its owner, find relief of pressure, and get a dopamine release. The "learning moment" might be even more reinforcing if he gets to graze.

In other words, horses don't discriminate between good and bad learning. They will search for the dopamine release regardless of how humans interpret their actions.

CHAPTER TWO

Messages travel through the brain electrochemically. Neurotransmitters are substances that aid in transmitting these impulses between two nerve cells or between a nerve and muscle. There are more kinds of neurotransmitters than one can imagine and researchers continue to find new ones. However, we will be most concerned with just some of the major neurotransmitters specific to movement, rewards, emotions, growth, and learning.

Axons are like long superhighways carrying numerous individual nerve fibers. Many of these axons are wrapped in myelin. The speed of the nerve transmission relies on the special myelin insulation around the fibers.

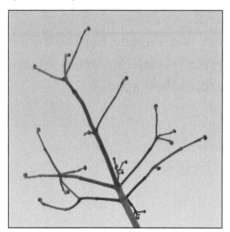

As nerves or neurons grow, they look much like trees without leaves. The nerve cell would be the trunk of the tree and the arms that branch off the nerve cell are called dendrites and actually look like branches on a tree.

These branches or dendrites are new roads to allow information/nerve transmission to travel in new directions, often crossing dendrites of other nerve cells. The more dendrites coming off a cell, the more pathways we have for information to travel in various directions.

The sprouting of these dendrites is called arborization because of its tree-like growth of nerve fibers. As we will learn later, stimulation and learning creates greater arborization (more roads of communication). Those nerve cells that receive little stimulation are often sparse with just a few branches. On a larger scale, the fewer dendrites, the less options cells have for transmitting information.

At the very end of dendrites are small bud-like structures called synapses. Nerve impulses are passed from one nerve cell to another through these synapses by the release of neurotransmitters. Once released, the neurotransmitter is received by a receptor at the end of the nerve branch of another nerve cell in close proximity. A heavy population of dendrites or nerve branches provides more opportunities for the transmission of neurotransmitters from one nerve to another (synapses).

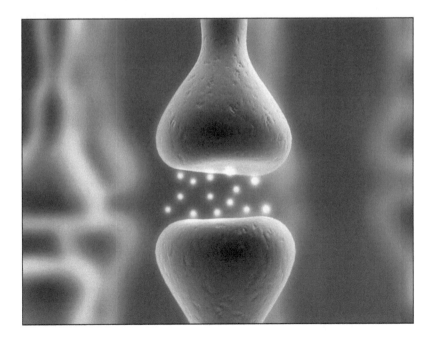

The receptors on the end of the nerve branch receiving the neurotransmitter are specially designed to accept that particular neurotransmitter and then will convert it into a nervous impulse and continue to send the message down the line through its synapses. For example, brains have opiate receptors that are specifically designed to capture endorphins.

Even before the foal is born, there is an organization and development occurring from the branching of dendrites, growth of synapses, and axonal connections that will play a key role in the brain's growth and maturation as well as the development of future brain functioning.

CEREBELLUM

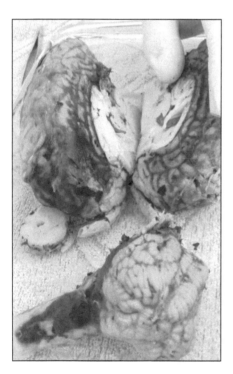

The horse's brain is about the size of a large grapefruit. The cerebellum is about the size of a large tangerine. It represents about one third of the horse's brain. Its relative size represents its importance. (In humans, the cerebellum represents only a fifth of the brain's overall size.)

In this photo of a horse brain dissection, Dr. Peters has removed the cerebellum (in foreground, with spinal cord attached) from the back of the brain.

The horse is largely a motor/ sensory animal and the cerebellum is vital in its connection with these systems. Its significance is reflected by the fact that the cerebellum receives its deposition of myelin soon after initial myelination of the motor and sensory roots. One sees the foal's neurodevelopment as its jerky movements become smooth, i.e., as the cerebellum and its connections are developed.

The cerebellum takes in and integrates sensorimotor information to produce smooth and well- coordinated movement. The cerebellum will directly perceive and adjust to the sensation of pressure on the horse's legs and trunk and will react by coordinating the horse's voluntary movement. The cerebellum gauges and measures timing and contraction of opposing muscles needed for smooth movement. It completes this task by unified control of all the complicated inputs from the spinal cord, brainstem, and brain.

The cerebellum and the vestibular (balance) systems control head posture and coordination. These areas respond to sensory information coming in from the head, limbs and trunk. The horse needs to use its head in order to balance its body and this need is especially true when keeping balanced with a rider on its back. Therefore, one needs to think about the impact of any of the various apparatus that restrict the horse's head (such as tiedowns).

In terms of the learning and storage of physical movements and motor routines, there is no more important structure than the cerebellum. Indeed, it is the library where learned motor routines are stored. The hippocampus, the structure typically associated with memory, is not required for remembering motor and sensory information gradually acquired through repetition.

The horse's brain is truly wired for routines.

Motor routines run through the **cerebellum –>> basal ganglia ->> orbitofrontal region**. There is no large frontal lobe in horses.

The frontal lobe is where we as humans perform abstract thinking, organize things, categorize things, and multi-task. It is responsible for a large part of our human personality. There is not much brain area dedicated to this type of thinking in the horse.

Horses don't do well categorizing. For example, a donkey is a four-legged, hooved animal that resembles a horse, but most horses are fearful of them in their first encounter. Horses also have difficulty generalizing from one thing to the next such as a tarpaulin of a different color or in a different place.

The basal ganglia sits deep in the middle of the brain and plays a key role in initiating and coordinating movement. It contains a high percentage of neurons that use dopamine as their neurotransmitter.

Dopamine is the neurotransmitter associated with motor movement. It aids in the transmission of information across neurons involved in complex motor movements.

In humans, it is the lack of dopamine in this same system that results in Parkinson's disease, characterized by difficulty initiating movement, poor balance and jerking, shaking movements.

Dopamine is also a very rewarding substance in the brain and is highly reinforcing.

Positive feedback is key to the learning process and the large percentage of dopamine neurons in the basal ganglia plays an important role in learning related to feedback and reward. The basal ganglia receives overlapping inputs from sensory and motor areas. These inputs result in dopamine reinforcement for associating stimulus with response. This phenomenon suggests that habit-learning happens when dopamine reinforces synaptic changes in nerves activated just before the reward was presented.

The cerebellum and basal ganglia are responsible for procedural learning. Learned motor skills are embedded in procedures that are played out in the horse's performance. In this system, motor learning can occur without any awareness that learning is taking place.

In brain imaging studies on humans, investigators have found that several areas of the brain are activated when learning a motor sequence. Sensory and motor areas of the brain are activated as well as the basal ganglia. Functional MRI shows that practicing will recruit additional neurons in motor areas of the brain. Motor skill learning creates changes in nerve circuits that become dedicated to performing the task. Early on, larger areas of the brain are needed such as attention and awareness but they become less important as the task becomes more routine. When we learn to drive, we are very alert and aware of everything we do and everything around us. But eventually we drive almost in automatic pilot.

In horses and humans, the cerebellum is also important in these early stages of motor learning. It ensures that the specific order of movements are coordinated and executed with the proper timing. The cerebellum stores the skill-based information in long-term motor memory.

Someone once asked baseball great Yogi Berra whether the pitcher had thrown him a curveball or fastball that he had hit solidly for a home run. Berra said, "I don't know, I can't hit and think at the same time." In this example, constant practice hitting fastballs and curveballs provided various motor memory programs that allowed Berra to select and adjust to whichever pitch was thrown without consciously having to think about it. He was using procedural programs relying on his cerebellum and basal ganglia.

Humans may struggle initially when learning motor tasks because they are often thinking too much. It is the frontal lobe that overanalyzes and critiques. We think: "okay, now remember, eyes ahead, feet shoulder-width apart, keep the elbow elevated, weight back" and "gee, I hope I don't look like a fool."

The horse has none of these thoughts because it lacks a developed frontal lobe.

Horses become comfortable learning motor patterns. The patterns give them a greater repertoire of consistent and predictable motor responses in dealing with their environment.

As we will learn later, horses need to be in the right emotional and neurochemical state of arousal for learning to occur. Once they've established a pattern of dopamine-reinforced learning, they become quite masterful at finely discriminating what behaviors get rewarded. Their responses then become faster and more accurate. With greater understanding of what is being asked of them without undue or excessive pressure, they learn to respond to finer and finer cues. At this point, it appears that they have learned to learn and can grasp or process more complicated behavioral requests more quickly.

It has also been shown that horses who are allowed to learn and problem-solve grow more dendrites, have greater arborization and produce more synaptic connections. In other words, they grow bigger and better connected brains with greater mental flexibility.

THALAMUS

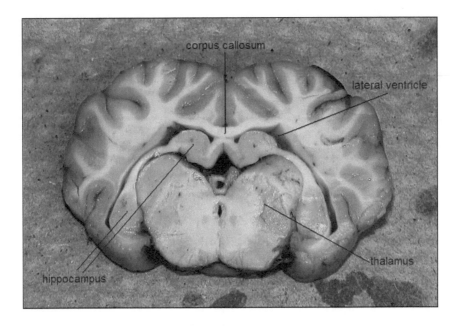

Most brain message traffic is routed through the thalamus. It is like a major airport through which flights are routed and sent to their destinations. Or like a telephone operator, where calls (information) are collected and then sent out to their specific location (phone of the person called). It is an egg-shaped structure located deep in the center of the brain, with its location denoting its importance.

The thalamus is also situated at the top of the brainstem so that it can process information coming up through the spine and brainstem and send this information to its proper location in the brain. A part of the thalamus called the reticular-activating system detects brainstem messages and plays a key role in providing arousal and initiating attention.

The basal ganglia, the structure discussed earlier which plays a key role in motor functioning, sits adjacent to the thalamus on each side.

HYPOTHALAMUS

The hypothalamus, as its name implies (hypo= below), sits below the thalamus. Its most important function is acting like a thermostat to create a set point or homeostasis. It maintains the horse's physiological and emotional equilibrium and brings the **autonomic nervous system** under its control.

The autonomic nervous system controls such functions as heart rate, breathing, digestion, sweating, and chemical secretions. The horse's emotions (especially fear and aggression), memory, sense of smell, and motor functions all have connections that run through the hypothalamus. The hypothalamus is a key structure in activating the fight or flight response.

The autonomic nervous system is made of two divisions, the **parasympathetic nervous system** and **the sympathetic nervous system.** These two systems are driven by simple reflexes involving the spinal cord, brainstem (medulla), and hypothalamus. The parasympathetic system is related to neurons or nerve connections in the brainstem. The sympathetic nervous system is associated with nerve connections in the spinal cord.

Fear responses chemically activate the sympathetic nervous system stimulating the spinal cord through the hypothalamus and the brainstem to prime the horse for maximum physical response. Increased heart rate, dry mouth, constriction of pupils (where you can see white in the horse's eyes) and adrenaline surge are all indicators of the sympathetic nervous system at work.

The Mare and the Bottle

Martin Black:

When a horse is investigating something, they look, smell, feel with the whiskers, lips, then teeth. It is not uncommon for them to get a hold of an object in their teeth then get scared and tighten their jaw.

In the following pictures, this young mare decided to investigate a bottle that had some pebbles in it and a cord attached. Once she picked it up, she couldn't let go and she couldn't get away from the bottle. This rather violent attempt went on for over two minutes until her jaw muscles were exhausted and she weakened and dropped it.

This is not much different than a horse who gets scared and bucks with a rider when the rider pulls the reins to try to stop the horse. What can happen is the horse is already panicked and is trying to escape, then by pulling on the head we make the horse feel they can't get away which causes more panic. In some situations, a horse may only need a short distance to feel safe from their predator but when the uncertain situation follows them, they continue their fight for freedom.

Dr. Steve Peters:

In the previous series of pictures, Martin describes and documents a situation in which a young horse investigates and picks up a bottle. The movement and noise from a bottle activate the sympathetic nervous system resulting in a violent flight or fight response. As part of this response, the mare's jaws clamp down tightly so that she cannot release the bottle and escape the perceived threat. Only when the horse becomes fatigued is she able to relax her jaws enough to drop the bottle. At that point, the parasympathetic nervous system is activated and relaxation occurs.

The parasympathetic nervous system is all about relaxation. Some of its indicators are salivating, constriction of pupils (where the color of the horses eyes seem to make up the entire eye with almost no white) and in the closing and opening of the eyes rapidly (called the eye blink response).

The trigeminal nerve is a cranial nerve located near the pons (bridge between the spinal cord and brain) and has three branches. The trigeminal nerve is both a sensory and motor nerve. Its motor functions are related to biting and chewing and its sensory aspect is related to sensation in the face. The first of its three branches of nerve fibers runs to the upper eyelid and cornea of the eye, the second to the lower eyelid, nostril or nares and upper lip, and the third runs down the lower jaw to the lower lip.

Martin Black:

If we look at the bay horse in the center of this photo, the head is down and moving toward the horse to its left indicating a threat to the sorrel horse. The interesting thing in this photo: wrinkles in the jaw indicating the horse is clenching the jaw extremely tight. The cheeks and muzzle area also are very tight. The ears are laid-back at fairly extreme degree. It adds up to signs of anger or frustration. If we look at the passive expression from the sorrel horse, it can explain why the bay horse's expressions are so loud.

We can see the tightness around the muzzle area. But if we look close just below the noseband of the halter and on the upper left, and also between the mouth and the center of the nostril, we can see a tendon very tight just under the skin. It can be helpful to get familiar with these signs because they can express fear by tightening these tendons without showing any expression in other areas.

Dr. Steve Peters:

You may be familiar with seeing particular oral movements in the horse (such as lip-licking) that indicate their physiological state. For example, a response to stress will release adrenaline and lead to a relatively dry mouth. The horse starts licking with the return of saliva secretion when the balance of the sympathetic and parasympathetic chemical reactions return to their normal set point.

Hypothalamus

Martin Black:

Anybody who has worked with young horses is familiar with them licking their lips, and this is usually a good sign. Some people believe they lick their lips when they've learned something or when they're relaxed. I believe this is true in part, but I've seen horses kick somebody or buck somebody off and then lick their lips. They may have learned something and become relaxed, but it may not be a positive thing for us. What I have found to be consistent is when they are stressed and they become relaxed they will lick their lips. When they're stressed, their jaw muscles are tight and when they're relaxed, their jaw muscles are softer and the same is true of the lips and muzzle area.

So in the training process we may put pressure on them and they become tight and when they give us positive response we take away the pressure and they relax and lick their lips. This experience can be positive for both us and the horse. We just need to be aware of the situation leading up to them licking their lips and make sure we are getting a favorable response for them to learn from and not something that may be a good experience for them but a bad experience for us.

Horses have an amazing memory. They remember events. They remember places they have been. And they can remember experiences they've had with us extremely well. It can be a problem if there are things we would like them to forget that may be a negative thing in our program. When it happens it just means that we need to offset the bad experience with enough good experiences to outweigh the bad experiences. If the experience was bad they may only need a few good experiences to be comfortable in the situation again. But if it's a real traumatic experience, it may take 100 good experiences before they can be comfortable in the same situation. The good thing is that horses are extremely forgiving and they want to be comfortable. Once they get confident that they can avoid the trouble or that we will not get them in trouble, then they will be in a good frame of mind and easier to work with.

We may be at the same place and see the same thing as a horse and come away with a totally different impression of the experience. We may remember it as a very pleasant experience and the next time the horse is at the same place he may be terrified. For example, we could be in an arena and see a big American flag with a light breeze picking it up and popping the end of it. We may see this flag and think of what it represents and see how the breeze puts the waves in the flag and be emotionally moved in a good way. But the horse being naturally suspicious of loud noises and things above him moving quickly could be real scared of it. On top of that, we might not be paying attention to what's going on inside the horse's mind and we're holding the horse trying to keep him from leaving. The confinement could make him feel trapped and make him feel even worse about the experience. Years later we may revisit this arena with our horse and we may remember it as pleasant. But the horse may respond by being more scared than he seemed to be during the original experience.

This situation is an example of how we may not understand why the horse is reacting with fear when there is nothing that we can see for him to be afraid of. But in the horse's mind, he may think that something is going to jump out from behind the building or fall out of the sky and get him. Because he's nervous about this, you may have a hold of him which in his mind confirms that you are going to keep him confined and he will not be able to escape. So in his mind, it could be a life-threatening situation that he may not be able to escape and you see it as a quiet sunny day with nothing to worry about.

Horses are going to remember things differently than we do because they see things differently than we do. Because they are prey animals, they are wired to be on the lookout for things that may threaten them. It doesn't have to be a threatening experience. It can be the impression of a threatening experience that they remember. And because man is a predator and we see ourselves as superior to other life, we are not threatened. We think in terms of how we are going to conquer the situation.

AMYGDALA

The amygdala (translated as 'almond' due to its shape) is part of a primitive area of the brain called the limbic system. It rests on the tip of the hippocampus (The hippocampus, translated as 'seahorse,' is the structure most associated with memory as we usually think of it.).

The amygdala is involved in emotion, particularly fear and rage. In the horse, we define emotion as a mental state arising spontaneously rather than through a conscious effort. It is often accompanied by physiological changes. Emotion is NOT feeling sad, proud, jealous, or humble. It is more primitive and instinctual in the horse.

In animal studies, overstimulation of the amygdala has produced rage reactions.

The amygdala is involved in a system of circuits that allow it to send nerve impulses to the hypothalamus causing activation of the sympathetic nervous system and release of the chemical noradrenaline at the neuromuscular junctions to prepare the horse for movement. The circuitry also activates the reticular system of the thalamus (responsible for the level of alertness) making the horse hyper-alert and preparing it for physical readiness.

Martin Black:

This photo shows the horse restricted by the halter rope, but the ears are up analyzing information, although the eye is looking away for an escape. The important thing to notice here is that the muzzle is very soft and relaxed indicating that the horse is not afraid but rather annoyed, and at the same time confident of its escape.

This photo shows a horse working hard, ears back, head up, not worried, not happy, but frustrated.

As mentioned, the amygdala performs a primary role in the processing and memory of emotional experiences. The memory is consolidated with its emotional power. So the emotional response around the event influences the memory of that event. Animal studies do show that stress can create a stronger memory of an event.

We also know that in Post Traumatic Stress Disorder (PTSD) in humans, non-erasable memories or super memories can be permanently etched into one's memory. The abnormally intense stress and fear that create PTSD often result in realistic flashbacks in any situation similar to the original trauma. For example: a Vietnam veteran is walking on a Florida beach on a hot summer day. He hears a helicopter fly overhead. He looks up to see it through the leaves of palm trees. Suddenly, he feels as if he is transported back to Vietnam and that the trauma is reoccurring.

As in the above example, emotions of fear will last long beyond the initial physiological experience of fear. It is this re-looping through the amygdala that can reactivate the same level of fear responses at a later time when exposed to any stimuli which may have some similar connection for the horse to the original negative emotional experience.

FOREBRAIN

I use the term forebrain or primitive frontal lobe to speak about the front of the horse's brain. In human beings, our frontal lobes are extremely large. In fact, the greatest volume of myelinated circuitry in humans is in the frontal lobe. Our abstract ideas, our thinking process, our processing of information, and our personalities are all frontal lobe functions.

The horse does not possess this developed frontal lobe. Most all of the horse's neurocircuitry is designed to provide movement and coordination of its four limbs. The horse lacks the cognitive capability of having such thoughts as, "I know what this person wants me to do but today I don't feel like it," or "I'll pull a fast one on this guy and have a good chuckle at his expense."

However, because we <u>do</u> have a frontal lobe, we can create all kinds of imaginative things to attribute to our horse. Certainly, a lonely child who talks to an animal with big eyes and perked ears can say the horse is being a good listener and is the only one in the world who listens.

Someone with anger issues could attribute a horse's confusion, fear, or self-preservation as insubordination and deserving of punishment. Horses are horses and behave as horses should. They have no alternative. It's humans who decide to label certain of these behaviors as stubborn, lazy, or sour.

The horse's forebrain is much like a sparkplug acting to initiate voluntary action and movement. This initiation is a conscious one. Reward and pleasure may also have dedicated areas in the frontal region. Once the forebrain initiates movement, other systems takeover and control falls on the brainstem, cerebellum, and spinal cord.

We may fail to engage the forebrain in initiating movement in situations where the horse seems frozen (what one might label as 'uncooperative'). However, often if we get the horse to move in *any* direction, they seem to be able to get going again. This strategy is an example of bypassing the initiation of the forebrain and getting the horse to use a pre-established motor pattern.

Martin Black:

One of the hardest things for us to understand with horses is that they don't think like us. They have a very strong memory that we lack. But we have the power to reason and they do not.

Because of our reasoning power, we plan for the future, look at the calendar to plan things out, and save for our retirement. We are conscious of our appearance and what other people may think of us and all of these things are big factors in our decision making. None of these things affect horses' decision-making. They remember the past, live in the present, and make no plans for the future past bringing comfort to a current situation. We remember the past, live in the present, and based on knowledge we have gained, we plan for the future.

The horse can roll in the mud, have knots and trash in his mane and tail, and have no sense of embarrassment around the other horses. They may eat until they're content and give no thought at that point to where their next meal is going to come from. They are not going to guard some leftover hay from the other horses so they have something to eat later. Horses are not greedy. They don't have an ego. You can't shame or embarrass them. You cannot discipline them for what they've done in the past. They will only relate to the current situation. They don't have a sense of humor. They don't play jokes on each other. In so many ways they just process things differently than we do. It's not a matter of being smarter or dumber, it's just understanding that they are different. We like to think of ourselves as more intelligent but sometimes it is very hard for people to understand. Once we understand they think differently, and how they think differently, then we can be a lot better prepared to communicate with them.

CHAPTER THREE

SENSES

Horses are motor sensory creatures. Their brains tell us so. The brain area in which sensations are processed is referred to as the **somatic sensory cortex**. If we consider the somatic sensory cortex as a map, its largest areas would represent the most sensitive body areas because these brain areas are most densely-packed with sensory nerves.

If we use the United States as an example, the mouth and lips represent Alaska. The flank, withers, groin and bulbs of the heels represent California, Texas, Montana, and Wyoming. The horse's chest, although physically rather large, represents a very small state like Delaware in our analogy.

Information from sensory receptors in the muscles, joints, skin, mouth, teeth, and abdomen are all processed in the somatic sensory cortex. However, the primary somatic sensory cortex does <u>not</u> play a critical role in processing painful stimuli. Pain is processed through the thalamus.

Sensory receptors either have a tissue capsule covering the nerve or are bare nerve endings. Receptors with bare nerve endings are called nociceptors (noci-translates as harm or injury). These nociceptors are activated by painful stimuli and many of them have fine, free nerve endings in the skin. These nociceptors are not only sensitive to noxious stimuli

but can activate higher threshold sensory pain fibers, informing the horse that tissue damage may be occurring. Pain nociceptors can be fast-firing for a pricking, jabbing pain or slow-firing for burning pain.

Processing this painful stimuli is through the thalamus. The thalamus has connections to the amygdala involving the circuitry for emotional responses to the pain. Horses appear to be particularly affected by their level of emotional arousal. They become hypersensitive to a stimulus known to cause them pain. The thalamus also plays a role in localizing the pain and measuring its intensity.

Encapsulated receptors, those with a tissue capsule covering, are referred to as mechanoreceptors. These receptors, located in skin, detect light touch especially in particularly sensitive areas or they are located in deep tissue and detect deep pressure and vibration changes. These receptors are responsible for detecting touch and determining where the horse's limbs and body are in space (proprioception).

Certain touch receptors will quickly suffer fatigue and grow less sensitive in the horse. When the receptor continues firing, it quickly down regulates, becoming less and less sensitive to stimuli. In essence, receptor desensitization occurs. When we first put on a shirt or pair of pants, we only feel the cloth on our skin for a few moments before we are unaware of its touch on our entire body. The only time we notice the feeling of wearing clothes is when we remove them. In this situation, our touch receptors fire when our clothes make contact and then become deadened or desensitized, only firing again when the receptor is released (i.e., we take off our clothes). This phenomenon is likely occurring when the horse adapts to wearing a saddle.

The importance of down regulation in sensory cells and desensitization of the sensory receptors is that application of constant rein or leg pressure can deaden or habituate sensory information processing. Once the horse's skin receptors are overwhelmed, any response to lighter, subtle aids will be lost for a while.

When renowned horsemen warn against "not dwelling on the horses side with your leg," "quitting the rein with the slightest sign of yielding," and "any aid, even if it's correctly applied, will deaden the horse if used to excess," they have recognized this phenomenon.

Pain receptors or free nerve endings will also transmit impulses continuously for long periods of time, masking the horse's ability to detect and respond to a lighter sensory cue. Pain perception through the thalamus and activation of the amygdala may result in upregulating pain receptors and activating emotional responses that could escalate into increased sympathetic nervous system activation, creating full blown fight or flight.

If the horse is pushed or punished or if its stress level becomes too high when developing and learning motor patterns, it will have exceeded their set point. By backing off and allowing the horse to reset, for example, by taking a few extra laps around the round pen, their parasympathetic nervous system will become activated. Their heart rate will slow. Their arterial blood pressure will decrease and the parasympathetic sensory projection from the 9th cranial nerve, glossopharyngeal nerve, will reactivate the salivary glands (licking and chewing).

This horse's head is slightly elevated above the withers indicating a sense of alertness. The ears are soft but not in the same position. The eyes are very soft. The muzzle area is soft and the horse is licking its lips. These are all indications of a horse coming out of a more stressed frame of mind and into a more relaxed frame of mind. This look is very typical for a horse to have in the early stages of a learning experience.

By allowing horses to reset their set point, one will allow them to down regulate. They will become less sensitive over time to situations that once resulted in activation of the sympathetic nervous system.

When a horse is turned loose and trots or runs with a saddle, the stirrups will be flopping on its side. If it's the first time he's experienced this sensation, he could get scared. He can learn in a very short time to ignore or be desensitized to the feel of the stirrups moving on his side. The same is true under the same application of a person using their legs attempting to communicate with the horse. If our legs are used effectively, we can get a change in a matter of seconds. We can keep the horse sensitive and expecting to get away from the cue by performing our desired response.

On the other hand, if we continue the movement of our legs without getting a response, the horse can learn to accept or ignore the movement of our legs. Or, if the horse responds and is not rewarded, he will quit putting out the effort of a response. The more sensitive we are to the changes the horse makes and the more we reward him accordingly, the more sensitive the horse can be in his response.

If our intention is to continue the movement of our legs until we reach a desired speed and the horse only reaches half of the speed and he doesn't experience stronger leg movement, he may not have enough encouragement to put out any more effort, so he will quit. Or, if we continue the movement of our legs to keep the horse at a desired speed and he doesn't experience any change with our legs in relation to his performance, he will also learn to ignore the movement of our legs.

Key senses

Like people, horses send a lot of messages with their facial expressions and body language. The positioning of their neck and head, the movement of their ears and eyes, and the tightness around the muzzle area are all strong indicators of their state of mind.

Vibrissae

Microscopic image of the nerve within a vibrissa

The vibrissae are stiff, hair-like sensors growing out of the skin around the horse's eyes and muzzle. They have their own distinct nerve and blood supply. These nerve fibers are densely packed and fire with incoming sensory information when an object brushes against them. There appear to be areas in the sensory regions of the brain dedicated to these vibrissa.

These sensory organs act as feelers in the horse's environment to help protect the vital areas of the eyes, ears, and lips by detecting things which may be in the horse's blind spots or too close for visual focus. Cosmetically trimming these sensors increases the risk of eye trauma and puncture wounds to the lips, muzzle and nostrils. Often when the horse appears to be sniffing or smelling something very closely, they are actually investigating the item by using the vibrissae. They can use these sensors much in the way a human would manipulate an item with their hands to assess it by feel.

Horses are extremely sensitive. They can feel something touch the end of their hairs on their body and respond. They use the whiskers on their muzzles regularly to investigate and analyze things they are unfamiliar with. We can present a bit to go in their mouth in a way that is threatening to them and they will tighten their lips and avoid opening their mouth. If they can be successful in moving away from us, they can learn to move away as we touch the first whisker. On the other hand, if we can present it in a non-threatening way, they can feel with their lips and investigate it. They can take it in their mouth to play with it and they can become very easy to bridle to the point they will reach for it and take it in their mouth like they are taking a treat from us.

If we are going to investigate whether an object is dry or wet, soft or hard, light or heavy, hot or cold, we could not do this by smelling it, looking at it, or listening to it. We would have to touch it, and we would probably touch it with our fingertips, then pick it up. In a second, we could analyze all the above features of this object. The horse has no fingertips. His hooves would not give him much of a sense of any of these features.

But when a horse wants to investigate something, they will first process it visually, then smell it, then they touch it with their whiskers. Sometimes this can be overlooked and we think the horse is smelling an object when actually it already smelled it several feet away. What they are doing is feeling the object with the end of their whiskers. After they are satisfied with the information they got from feeling it with their whiskers, then they may rub it with the fuzzy hair on their lips, then contact it with the tissue of their lips, then they may take it between their teeth, and may even take it in their mouth and feel with their tongue. Through this process they can determine the differences in an object. The whiskers can play just as big a role as anything else in processing the information for their investigation.

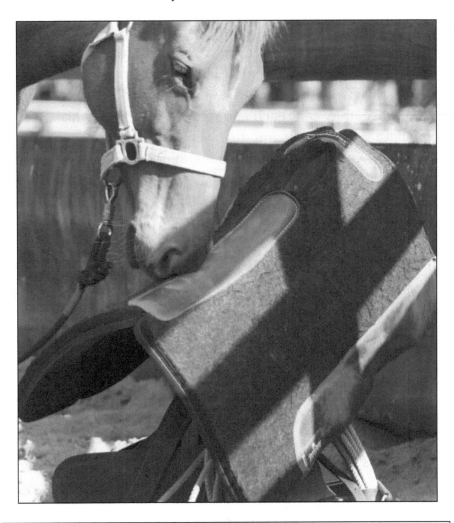

These photos could be mistaken for the horse smelling a blanket when in fact the horse smelled it from some distance. The horse's expression is relaxed which means he's not threatened and we can see from the position of the halter rope that the horse is at the blanket of his own free will. The horse shows all signs of exercising its curiosity and is using its muzzle area to feel the blanket as we would with our fingertips.

They also use these whiskers to help with their depth perception because they cannot see directly off the end of their nose. They have a good idea by looking at something how far it is from their mouth. But as they lose sight of it under their nose, they can reach and touch it with their whiskers to regulate when their mouth will actually make contact. Whiskers can help them prevent injuries to the eyes and muzzle area from objects such as a nail sticking out from a wooden manger.

This photo is of horses not only smelling each other but feeling each other with the muzzle area to get a better sense and to get to know each other better. We can see the horse on the left is more confident by his head being in a more natural position, and the horse on the right not showing as much confidence by reaching out with its nose reserving the opportunity to retract if it felt threatened.

Vision

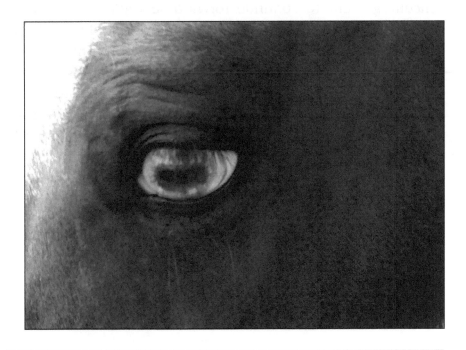

An eye wide open with wrinkles above it and with the eyelid blinking rapidly could indicate an alert horse interested in something and be a positive sign for us, or it could indicate a frightened horse that could be a negative sign for us. But taking into account what the ears, muzzle, and other indicators may tell us, we can determine what the horse may be thinking.

I had an experience where I was riding in the dark in two feet of snow one night. It was overcast, so there was no moon or starlight and not even the silhouette of the horse's head could be seen against the snow. We were traveling on a road but could not see the brush at the edge of the road and had to trust our horses to bring us home. I did have a sense of distance as we traveled and knew that we were coming to a cattle guard that was across the road under the snow. Our horses came to a sudden stop and refused some encouragement to continue forward so I got off and felt under the snow with my foot and found the rails of the cattle guard just a couple strides in front of my horse. They knew under two feet of snow that there were steel rails covering a deep hole that they would get tangled in and they stopped clear of it. Feeling my way to the end of the cattle guard I found the gatepost but still could not see it as my hand was touching it.

At the time, my vision tested well above average and yet I was as good as blind and the horses seemed to be able to get along as well as if it was daylight. We cannot ask the horse to verbally read a chart and it may be difficult to assess exactly how superior their vision is to ours. But in the dark or light they are able to see things that we cannot.

Vision is one of the horse's most important survival mechanisms. The horse's vision is designed to give it a wide panoramic view of the horizon. In essence, the horse has 350°

vision. There are small blind spots directly under the horse's head and between the eyes up around the forehead. The horse has a somewhat larger blind spot directly behind his tail. Because the eyes are set wide apart on each side of the head, most of what the horse sees is through monocular vision with one eye. Only when both eyes are looking at something does the horse have binocular vision.

Binocular vision is required for depth perception. Through movement of its head, the horse can bring both eyes to bear on an object. This design allows the horse to view the ground in front of them with binocular vision.

If you look at the horse's eye you'll note they have a horizontal pupil. This feature aids in their panoramic view, with each single eye able to see 180° horizontally.

In the human eye, there is a high concentration of photoreceptor cells (cones) packed together in the center of the retina. We might turn to look directly at something we pick up in our peripheral vision and perhaps squint to focus our vision. In horses, these ganglion cells (cones) are packed together horizontally in what has been termed the "lateral streak." It is this arrangement of highly packed cells that gives the horse its very narrow panoramic viewpoint.

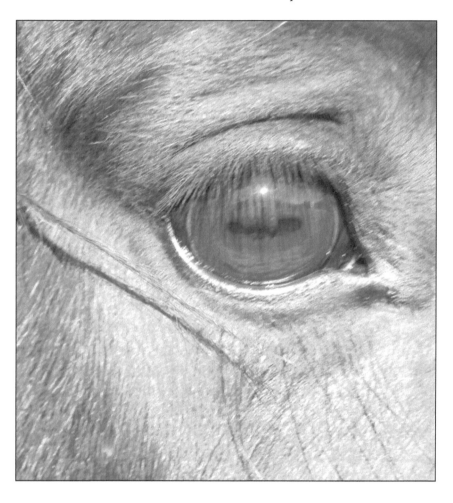

As stated earlier, the horse must move its head in order to bring things into focus. The horse can arch its neck sideways in order to put the object within the lateral streak. Horizontal vision in the horse is an ideal adaptation for scanning the horizon. In addition, the horse's eyes are geared to focus largely on objects in the distance. Their peripheral vision is adapted to detect motion such as a creeping predator.

The horse's ears at times appear to be connected to the horse's vision. Their ears tend to follow what they see. Often horses will keep their heads down while eating as their ears continue to scan like radar. If they detect something through their hearing, they will often stop chewing. If the potential threat calls for further investigation, they will raise their heads and freeze stock-still, staring straight ahead in the general direction of the sound.

There is circuitry to provide connections from the horse's eyes to the thalamus and hypothalamus. It can jolt the horse immediately into a flight response, stimulating adrenaline to the hypothalamus and stimulating motor flight through the thalamus.

It has been mistakenly stated that the horse has two brains. This misconception is largely due to the fact that horses may spook on one side after having been desensitized on the other. In actuality, the horse has one brain. However, visual signals are independently attached to the right and left thalamus. These independent visual signals will be processed through the hypothalamus and are instant triggers for the flight response. Therefore, the horse will be jolted into immediate flight reaction by these direct connections to the adrenal glands that activate control over motor function.

This reaction occurs far too quickly to rely on thinking. The horse spooks on the opposite or untrained side because of the independent connections of the optic nerves. Evolution has determined that a horse who spends too much time in thought will be eaten.

As previously noted, stress, anxiety, and panic can be detected in the horse's eye. The sclera or white area is opened wider in panicked animals as they attempt to draw in more visual information. A fixed eye may be indicative of stress of a more chronic nature.

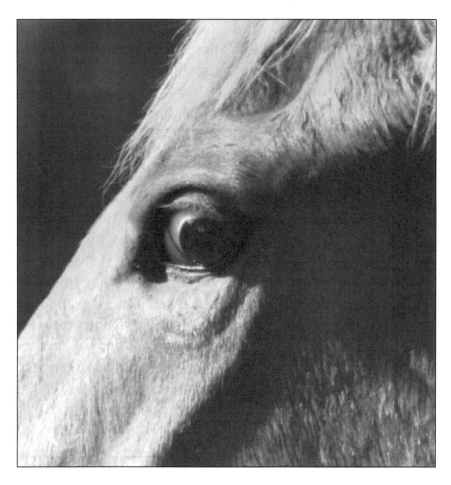

Because horses cannot change the shape of the lens of their eye, they compensate by moving their head. Therefore, when horses are forced by their rider to keep their heads stationary, they become more dependent on the rider to adjust to obstacles. Horses often try to flex their head when going over jumps. They are at the mercy of their rider if they are not allowed to judge for themselves. Accidents are often the result of restricted head movement.

Rods and cones are types of photoreceptors in the eye that convert light into signals. Rods are associated with night vision and triggered by low light levels. Rods discern things in black and white. Horses have excellent night vision due to a 20:1 ratio of rods to cones.

Another aspect of the horse's night vision is the tapetum. It is a reflective layer of cells that helps them capture more light. Animals with this adaptation have eyes that reflect back when headlights or flashlights are shone at them.

The cones require a bright light to produce a signal and are responsible for our color vision. Horses detect fewer colors than humans and have more difficulty seeing in bright light.

The horse also has a protective membrane that covers the eye to protect it from dust, dirt, and other objects. Occasionally referred to as the third eyelid, one can often see it when the horse uses it like a windshield wiper, pulling it down over the eye.

Hearing

The horse's outer ears can move independently like satellite dishes. These funnel-shaped cups capture and channel sound into the inner ear. The external ears each have 10 different muscles that allow them to move 180° and independently of each other. The horse has binaural hearing. They hear sound in both ears to locate the direction and distance of the sound. Very small differences in the time that the sound wave is captured by each ear allows the horse to gauge which ear first picked up the sound. This feature gives the horse a general sense of the sound's direction. The amplitude of the sound helps it to judge distance. Being a prey animal, the horse is prepared to flee in the opposite direction. Horses hear a wide range of high-frequency sounds such as a snapping branch stepped on by a predator. Horses often appear jumpy and nervous on a windy day especially in the fall when the wind will rustle the leaves. In this situation, the horse can be overwhelmed by the constant bombardment of auditory stimuli, making one of its chief survival mechanisms ineffective. This overload may cause the horse to be ever more vigilant in the use of its other senses and to compensate by preparing to respond with a flight response much sooner than would normally be the case.

Here is a horse utilizing his sense of hearing by his ears being forward, his head elevated and at an angle that gives his eyes the best visibility. It means he's interested but not threatened by what he's focusing on because his muzzle area is not tight and his nostrils are not wide open.

Smell

Smell is a very primitive sense and registers quickly in the horse's brain. The olfactory system is the one sense that does not have to be processed through the thalamus. It has its own connections to the brain. The olfactory bulbs in a horse are quite large in comparison to a human. The human's olfactory bulb may look like a shoestring lying against the undersurface of the frontal lobe. The horse's olfactory bulb looks more like the tongue of the shoe and covers a vast amount of the underside of the front of the horse's brain.

Smell is the horse's primary means of recognition. Giving the horse an opportunity to smell unfamiliar objects can help to reduce sympathetic arousal. Far too often, humans do not give the horse enough time to perceive objects by smell and to become comfortable with an unknown odor.

Horses will often loudly produce forced exhalations which sound like a snorting when unsure or sympathetically aroused. They do this in order to clear the nasal passage and to ready the nasal cavity to take a rich sample of the airborne molecules. Smells are turned into neural impulses by chemical receptors located in the nasal tissue.

Horses also have what is called a vomeronasal organ which features long tubes that line the mucous membranes. The tubular vomeronasal organs work by expanding and contracting like a pump when stimulated by certain odors such as pheromones in urine driving their contents to their destination. In fact, the horse will often produce a flehman response - an upward curling of the upper lip that helps to trap pheromones in the vomeronasal organ for further and closer analysis.

Horses have a much better sense of smell than people. For example walk around with a blindfold smelling different horses and try to identify them. It's not that the horse can't see or talk to each other, they're just aware of each other's smell. The average person cannot do this unless they're familiar with the heavy perfume or cologne another person is wearing.

Often a person makes the mistake of thinking horse are smelling something when they are actually wanting to feel it with their whiskers. An example would be when we approach a horse and it reaches with its nose to touch our hand or a saddle blanket so we stop and let it smell. Of course, its nose is touching us and it may be a little scared so the ribs are tight and it is taking short quick breaths. It appears the horse is smelling. Actually it smelled the blanket and us from several feet away if not from across the corral. As we approach they want to feel it, so we stop to give horses time to analyze and then they're satisfied and somewhat relaxed. Then we try to continue approaching at the side and they resist our approach and reach with the nose again because we allowed them to be comfortable and get relief by waiting while we were in front of them.

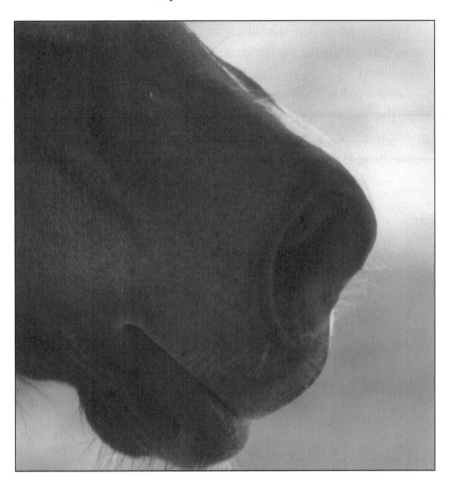

The person thinks the horse wants to smell it again when actually they're just wanting the relief they found earlier. They can see better with both eyes when we are in front of them. They have a greater sense of defense when we are in front of them so we are helping to satisfy their needs. They cannot see as well out of one eye and cannot defend themselves as well if we are at the shoulder. So in this common scenario, the horse is finding a place he's comfortable defending himself from the unknown and it has very little if anything to do with their need to smell.

The large round nostril means the horse is taking in all the air it can. It could be for one of two reasons: the horse has exhausted its oxygen supply in which case the lips would be relaxed as this photo indicates. The other reason would be that the horse may not be exhausted but is taking in large quantities of air, analyzing through its sense of smell something it may be threatened by.

CHAPTER FOUR

FEAR RESPONSE

Martin Black:

Here's a horse extremely panicked but not to the point that it is unaware of the boundaries of the corral. It is making some extreme maneuvers to try to escape the saddle. Anytime a horse panics it could be extremely dangerous for us and possibly for the horse. In this series of photos the horse is unable to predict where the next threat from the saddle is going to come from so the horse cannot predict what direction it's going to go next. It could be challenging for most people to stay safe whether on the horse's back or close enough to have hold of a lead rope on the ground.

This is a horse that is restricted by the halter rope, the ears indicate confusion, the eyes looking for an escape, the muzzle very tight indicating fear.

This horse is restricted by the halter rope, with the tight muzzle showing signs of fear, the ears showing signs of confusion, and if we look closely we see the lower eyelid with the wrinkles below it. The eye may open up more but it is not a sign of alertness as much as it is a sign of annoyance.

This horse is restricted by the halter rope and if we look at the poll we can see it has the horse's head tipped to the left giving the left eye better vision, and the left ear pointed left, with the muzzle area being somewhat soft indicates less fear and more confidence in the horse to make an escape to the left.

A strong sensory level of fear in the horse can result in a hyper-alert state with a pronounced exaggerated startle response. Lower levels of fear can be desensitized through repetition and learning. To some degree, experience may create a "down regulation" where some receptors in the brain become less sensitive. In this case, it takes more pressure to trigger a response.

Basically, down regulation involves getting used to something. As a horse gradually becomes familiar with something and can account for it and develop a behavioral response to it, there is less emotional reaction. On a neurochemical level, the horse's system has adjusted to the amount of neurochemicals which once created a fear response. After such an adjustment, it would now require a much greater degree of fear in order to produce the chemical reaction of a fear response.

When the horse is in a hyper-alert mode, its hearing becomes more acute and certain sensory inputs such as sudden movements or loud noises will trigger a flight response. When they are in this state, it is more difficult to capture their attention. Anything perceived as less important than the threat is ignored.

At a certain intensity of fear, the horse's behaviors fall under the influence of a chemical cascade of activity through systems designed to mobilize the horse to flee or fight. These reactions are determined by the release of specific neurotransmitters that influence the horse's behavior. Epinephrine/adrenaline and Norepinephrine/noradrenaline are neurotransmittors released by the adreno-medullary system to respond to stress.

Fear responses will activate the sympathetic nervous system. In most situations where the horse can escape, the result will be a strong flight or bolting response.

The amygdala is critical for emotional processing. The amygdala sends impulses to the hypothalamus. The hypothalamus acts as an emotional and physiological thermostat designed to maintain the horse at an equilibrium. However, when an instinctive reaction is required, the hypothalamus chemically activates the sympathetic nervous system via its connections to the thalamus. The thalamus, in turn, is involved in the brainstem reticular activating system. Breathing, arousal, and movement are all influenced by this activation of the sympathetic nervous system.

Sympathetic, adrenal, and medullary pathways are sometimes referred to as the SAM axis. The sympathetic nervous system increases arterial blood pressure, increases heart rate, dilates the pupils, puts the digestive system on hold, dries the mouth and opens up blood vessels supplying the muscles. The tight lips and enlarged pupils are part of the sympathetic activation of the sensory component of the trigeminal nerve. The adrenal medula is stimulated to release adrenaline. The medullary piece involves the brainstem and spinal cord. This almost immediate chemical reaction is preparing the horse for maximum physical response.

Should the fear be so intense that the horse becomes, in essence, chemically overwhelmed, the animal may be unable to process any incoming information. At this point, the horse may simply run through doors, fences, or into trees.

A secondary process that follows the more acute fear reaction involves the connection between the hypothalamus and pituitary gland. The hypothalamus will chemically stimulate the pituitary gland to release **cortisol.** Cortisol is a stress-related hormone. It can be found in the blood plasma of stressed horses. It gives the horse endurance to cope with chronic stress.

I think there are different levels of fear in a horse that we need to consider. When a horse panics, it is in a reactive state. Instincts take over and it doesn't give any thought to its actions. The horse learns very little if anything in this state of mind because it's going off instincts. A horse can be uncomfortable but not panic and it considers different options before responding. This state of mind is more productive for training purposes. Horses do not like panic, fear, or discomfort and they try to avoid these things. They seek the relaxed, comfortable state of mind. But when they are in a comfortable state all the time they lose their awareness of it, therefore it's the transition from the discomfort to comfort that gives them the awareness and appreciation. This awareness can become refined to the point that a thought of being uncomfortable is enough to motivate them to seek and appreciate the comfort.

Horses by nature are suspicious of many things including man. God designed them this way for their survival. We can use this natural suspicion or fear when working with them and help them find comfort in the response we are asking of them. We can regulate the discomfort far away from the panic (where they may shut down) and keep them in a state of mind that they are considering other options and help them make the right decisions. This process can feel good to them and they will want to repeat it. The more experience they get in the early stages of making these decisions and having good experiences doing them the easier it becomes for them. As they get older, it's not a matter of getting the pressure to get the response we want but rather seeking relief by their thoughts lining up with ours through practice in decision-making, experiencing different situations and patterns that we have done repeatedly with them.

Horses learn through repetition but I don't think it has to be limited to some simple basic maneuvers or a handful of patterns. They are so much more sensitive and intelligent than we are aware of but because we are intelligent in other ways, we may think of them as inferior. The fact is, they are so much more tuned into us because of them being a prey animal than we are tuned into them. There's a lot of missed opportunity to acknowledge their sensitivity and open lines of communication. They are very capable of acknowledging the slightest gestures we make and responding accordingly and by realizing this sensitivity and directing them to a comfortable place and a favorable place for us. Through repetition in this nature, they can be limitless in their performance.

LEARNED HELPLESSNESS

In classic scientific studies, animals quickly learn they can avoid adverse stimuli by performing a certain behavior. Often studies were arranged with an animal standing on an electric grid. A stimulus such as a light came on, followed by an electric shock of half of the grid. The animal soon learned it could avoid the shock if it jumped to the other half of the grid as soon as the light bulb was illuminated.

Next, the entire grid was electrically stimulated and the animal received a shock when the light went on, no matter what it did. In these studies, the animals often stopped responding and became passive. Many of them simply whimpered and shut down.

When horses find that no matter how they respond they cannot escape from pain or adverse stimuli, they may initially respond with fight or flight responses. When these responses are ineffective and produce no release no matter how they respond, they are at risk for developing learned helplessness.

Learned helplessness is a passive response to a chronically stressful situation that the animal finds inescapable. Horses may respond by initially doing what was asked of them in the past and resorting to previously learned patterns of stimulus and response. But under chronic stress that they cannot relieve by any predictable action, they withdraw, disengage, show little reaction, and appear quiet. These horses appear almost lifeless and often have fixed or sunken eyes.

Although these horses appear calm on the surface, their physiological functioning and cortisol levels would show they are unhealthy. There are lasting biological consequences to their state of distress above and beyond being unable to escape pain at the moment.

When horses are unable to escape pain, it may be a good evolutionary strategy to appear calm and passive so as not to draw the attention of predators looking for weak herd members that appear to be vulnerable, injured, or in pain.

Horses that don't feel well either from lack of nutrition or hydration or horses that are in pain will have signs of learned helplessness. A sore back, sore muscles, flesh wound, skin irritation, things that may not be expressed by lameness or obvious signs may go unnoticed if we are not aware of the emotional state of the horse. For example, a young horse who would ordinarily be running and playing may look depressed. And yet an older horse that may not get around real well may have a bright eye and put out a little effort to buck and play. So knowing what horses look like given the opportunity or environment to be happy, and seeing horses whose emotional well-being has been ignored can show us the subtle differences that will give us an insight to the horse.

Some of the old-style of breaking horses used the principle of breaking a horse's spirit, or teaching them learned helplessness by putting them in a situation where they could not find comfort and could not protect themselves and they learned to accept things as they were as a means of survival. Some modern round penning techniques that exhaust the horse by running them around, along with a desensitizing process, can basically have the same effect on the horse.

CHAPTER FIVE

The Physiological Bases of Learning and Memory in Training

Experiences change the horse; encounters with their environment alter behavior by modifying the nervous system. Learning refers to the process by which these experiences change the nervous system and therefore behavior.

We like to refer to these changes as memories. However, these learned experiences are not "stored" as much as they physically change the structure of the nervous system, altering neural circuits that participate in perceiving and performing.

The primary function of learning is to develop behaviors that are adapted to an ever-changing environment. The ability to learn permits horses to find food when they are hungry, shelter when they are cold or wet, and to seek the safety and companionship of herd members when they are alone. It also permits horses to avoid objects or situations that might harm them.

There are several types of learning that can influence the horse including: perceptual learning, stimulus–response learning, motor learning, and relational learning.

Perceptual learning is the ability to recognize stimuli that have been perceived before. Unless the horse learns to recognize something, it cannot learn how it should behave with respect to it. Therefore, it won't profit from experiences with it, and profiting from experience is what learning is all about. This process is largely a sensory function as horses learn to recognize things by visual appearance, sounds they make, how they smell, and how they feel. Perceptual learning is accomplished primarily by changes in the Sensory Association Cortex of the brain.

Stimulus-response learning is the ability to perform a particular behavior when a particular stimulus is present. It involves the establishment of connections between circuits involved in perception and those involved in movement. The behavior could be an automatic response such as a defensive reflex, or could be a complicated sequence of movements learned previously.

Motor learning is actually a component of stimulus-response learning. We can think of perceptual learning as the establishment of changes within the sensory systems of the brain. Stimulus-response learning is the establishment of connections between sensory systems and motor systems. And motor learning is the establishment of changes within motor systems.

A learning situation can involve varying amounts of several types of learning. For example, if we teach the horse to make a new response whenever we present a stimulus it has never seen before, it must learn to recognize the stimulus (perceptual learning) and then make the response (motor learning), while establishing the connection between these two new memories (stimulus-response learning).

In simple terms, neural circuits will detect a particular stimulus (perceptual system). Neural circuitry that controls a particular behavior (motor system) will produce a behavior that in turn becomes reinforcing (reinforcement system). This reinforcement is what strengthens the connection between the stimulus and response.

The major pathway between the sensory association areas of the brain and motor areas of the brain (required in motor learning) involves connections with the basal ganglia, cerebellum, and thalamus. Initially, the basal ganglia are passive "observers." But as learned behaviors become automatic and routine, those functions are transferred to the basal ganglia. It takes over the process (i.e., the horse no longer needs to think about what it's doing).

There is a neurological phenomenon called the **Hebb Rule.** When a cell is close enough to repeatedly excite an adjacent cell, a growth process or metabolic change takes place in both cells allowing for a more efficient information pathway that takes less powerful stimuli to excite in the future. It has thus been said: "neurons that fire together wire together."

Behavior is the product of the interaction of the horse's genes and its environment. As with all mammals, genetics only predispose the horse to behave in certain ways. Actual behavior on any occasion will be the result of a combination of predisposition and learned behavior in the environment or context. Learning can emphasize or suppress genetic tendencies. All equine behavior can be modified by experience. For example, learning can modify sex drive to the extent that a well-trained stallion behaves obediently around mares.

In general, people place too much emphasis on genetic predispositions and pay insufficient attention to any horse's learning potential. Vicious stallions, quarrelsome mares, and crazy horses that pull, shy, kick, or bite are not predisposed as such. Their behaviors are products of their experiences and training.

This horse's eye is wide open. Even though the lips are soft with the bit in the mouth, the rest of the muzzle area is tight. The head is elevated and the horse is expressing a slight degree of panic from being confined by the halter rope.

This horse has softened slightly in the muzzle area and eye from the previous photo and it is not resisting the halter rope. The horse is very alert and protective but not in a state of panic.

Once a horse has learned a behavior, it is important not to continue drilling the horse on that same behavior. Drilling will lead to habituation. Horses quickly become habituated to the girth, saddle, pulling on the bit, the rider's leg cues.

Overestimating the horse's mental ability leads to the assumption that the horse understands the training rather than simply responding to reinforcement. Training a horse within the anthropomorphic framework has potentially negative implications for the horse's welfare as well as the safety of riders. Horses that have been subject to inconsistent signals such as lack of release of pressure or pain often acquire the reputation for being difficult.

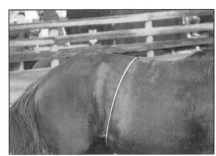 

Photos of horses being desensitized in preparation for the saddle

The lack of a developed frontal lobe in horses is adaptive for grazers because it allows for the formation of repetitive behavior patterns such as escape routines. The advantage of these habits over more reflective mental processes lies in their speed of acquisition and the immediacy and stability of reactions.

In other words, it doesn't pay to reason and contemplate. A horse is more likely to survive if it reacts by taking off at a gallop. For one thing, reasoning and similar brain functions burn a lot of calories. For another, those prey animals who pause to consider and contemplate may be eaten.

Hardwiring

The horse is born with the neural template for all the necessary instinctive behaviors that it will require throughout its life. In a sense, the horse's brain has the neural architecture of a ready-made, internalized structure of the external world. Neural pathways are predetermined.

The animal is born with the motor pattern to walk, trot, lope, do flying lead changes, suckle, startle at certain shapes, to be especially aware around water, caves and ditches and be pre-programmed for sex later in life. We call these features 'hardwired.' In training, the horse must learn to offer desirable learned responses which, under the control of humans, override instincts to run, eat, socialize, and copulate.

In the early stages of learning, associations form in the brain's simple, fragile pathways and networks. The more a particular response is practiced as a consequence of its eliciting stimulus, the more that neural network develops. After a number of repetitions, a repetitive behavior pattern forms. These learned responses modify instinctive drives and can override their expression.

Horses are highly motivated to seek freedom from confinement, pressure, or effort. Panic and fearful responses are often manifested by bolting, bucking, or rearing. Those actions are geared to obtain highly-rewarding freedom, a feeling that they have shed a predator from their back.

In their natural habitat or in certain domestic settings, horses are free to reduce pressures and reset their nervous system. In antagonistic encounters, they can compete to resolve disputes with other horses. When frightened, they can flee. If faced with hunger, they can search for and consume forage.

These issues will usually be resolved very rapidly. Domestic horses who cannot consistently obtain their freedom from pressures will often have to cope with the development of chronic stress.

Chronic conflict as a result of training manifests in situations where the horse receives constant pressure or pain. It can lead to greater and greater amounts of tension and a repressed flight response. Unable to escape pressure and depending on their makeup, horses may find that rearing, shying, or bucking become reinforcing, especially if these behaviors dislodge the rider.

In training situations, chronic states of stress and conflict increasingly emerge when an association between what we are asking of the horse and what is expected is not clear enough for the horse to understand. It is within this framework that most so-called problem horses develop. The more horses experiment with conflict behaviors and associate them with even occasional positive outcomes, the more likely they are to abandon their previously learned responses. They're driven by their hardwired instincts to escalate tension when they experience conflict.

A relaxed eye and relaxed ear can indicate the horse is not threatened and could be in a good frame of mind to learn something and be safe to be around.

CHAPTER SIX

PHYSIOLOGICAL and PSYCHOLOGICAL CONSEQUENCES of ENVIRONMENTS that BLOCK HORSES NORMAL & NATURAL BEHAVIORS

The horse is designed to move with a herd and eat continuously. Free-ranging horses can move an average of 15 miles a day with their social group. Horses will also spend an average of 16 to 17 hours a day grazing.

There is no longer any question that placing horses in environments unlike their natural habitats is harmful to the welfare of the horse. This position is not opinion. It is firmly based on an ever-increasing body of research.

I can recall how sad it was to visit a zoo in the 1960s where the big cats such as lions paced back and forth in small cement enclosures. Intelligent primates were in small cells with bars. Fortunately, zoos realized the physiological and psychological damage this type of management created. Enlightened zoo managers began to replicate natural environments for their animals. As a result, we've been able to see healthier animals do quite well when placed in habitats that allow them to behave and function in accordance with their natural design.

It is becoming common knowledge and shown by research that confining the horse and restricting its feeding to a few large meals each day causes neurosis and digestive problems.

Horses require the affiliation of other herd members and develop strong social bonds. Being social and sensory animals, and being in physical contact with other horses is necessary for their well-being. Grooming, play and communication require tactile (touch) interaction. With other horses standing guard, horses are comfortable enough to lie down.

There is also a strong body of research showing increased physiological stress reactions in confined and isolated horses. Simply housing horses together in separate stalls does not satisfy their need for sensory communication.

Taking locomotion away from the horse by confining it to a stall goes more against its nature as well. Locomotion is part of its innate survival mechanism required for a sense of well-being. Movement plays an important role in their digestive function.

Some common neuroses that develop in confined horses are weaving and pacing. Weaving is a tossing of the head back and forth almost like the horse's head movement while moving out at a brisk walk.

Repetitive behaviors related to blocked movement are called locomotor **stereotypies**. Locomotor stereotypies in captive animals are defined as repetitive, non-varying patterns of behavior that serve no obvious purpose or goal. Research data on captive animals shows that individual stereotypies appear to be based on the interruption of normal foraging behavior. Providing environments that allow for a more complete sequence of food-searching behaviors reduces these neurotic stereotypic behaviors.

Weaving has been linked to high levels of stress and anxiety and a reduction in serotonin (Serotonin is the brain chemical linked to stability of mood. Low levels of serotonin are seen in humans suffering from depression). Weaving and pacing in the horse appear to be poor substitutes for loss of free movement. The reduced serotonin levels suggest these horses are psychologically uncomfortable. These movements appear to be strategies to reduce stress and anxiety due to confinement, inability to graze, isolation, and a lack of companionship. Grazing itself is relaxing to the horse.

Pacing is a common neurotic behavior in free-ranging animals who are confined. Anyone old enough to visit the lion cage at the zoo in the 1960's can attest to this phenomenon.

Horses can be very sensitive to the footfall and rhythm of horses around them as they travel and when they are turned loose. We can see horses in cadence with each other as they move out in the open and when they are close to each other for security. Horses like to be in rhythm with the rider on their back if we can offer them some consistency. A rider who does not have a lot of energy or rhythm will likely develop a horse that does not perform with a lot of energy. A rider with a lot of energy will likely develop a horse who performs with more energy.

GRAZING

Grazing with their head lowered to the ground is the preferred method of ingestion for horses. In fact, hanging hay nets above the ground and at eye level can result in eye trauma from stiff stalks or sticks and can contribute to COPD (Chronic Obstructive Pulmonary Disease). COPD is a common lung and respiratory problem in confined horses breathing in large amounts of small airborne particles. Horses are far more likely to inhale these airborne particles when feeding from hay nets or wall racks.

There are also high rates of colic and ulcers in confined horses. The horse is an herbivore, physiologically designed to graze continuously. Its digestive system requires fiber or roughage. The horse's stomach is not designed to be empty. The stomach is always filled with gastric acid secretions.

Continuous grazing means plant material enters the stomach steadily. It digests food quickly. Plant matter then moves slowly through the horse's long, twisting colon. Ideally, when the horse moves freely, the bowels are stimulated to process this fecal matter. If the horse is not allowed to move, they are more prone to colon impaction (i.e., colic).

Constant eating also produces salivation. Horses salivate when they chew. Salivation buffers the stomach through the production of bicarbonate. Research has shown that horses will chew hay at least four times as long as they will grain. More chewing produces much more salivation. Grain is absorbed and digested much more quickly than natural forage. Thus the stomach is empty for longer periods of time and prone to the caustic effect of gastric acidity on the stomach lining. An empty gut with less salivation diminishes the protective effect of bicarbonate and allows gastric acidity levels to become an increased risk factor for ulcers.

Even though feeding grain may provide nutritional benefit, it results in reduced chewing time and a more rapid passage through the stomach. Feeding grain also denies horses the opportunity to slowly graze at leisure. It denies the horse the opportunity to maintain constant gut fill. It not only interrupts digestive function but it interferes with natural behavioral and psychological components related to the ability to free graze.

Chewing and lip movements have been related to the parasympathetic nervous system and relaxation. Conversely, a tense mouth is associated with the sympathetic nervous system and alarm or agitation. Horses allowed to graze with a hay or pasture diet have significantly fewer digestive problems than horses fed intermittent large meals of grain.

Cribbing is a neurotic behavior seen in stalled or confined horses. It may initially start out as a behavioral attempt to produce more salivation in response to increased gastric acid secretions in the stomach. In cribbing, the horse bites onto a hard object like a stall door or fence with its incisors, then arches its neck and pulls back on the object to suck in air. Cribbing horses have a high rate of ulcers. Research does not support the idea that wind-sucking creates the ulcer as little air actually gets into the stomach.

Cribbing itself develops into an obsessive-compulsive behavior that releases pleasurable endorphins. This repetitive stereotypic behavior becomes highly reinforcing and the horse becomes addicted to the release of pleasure-producing endorphins in the brain.

As with treating obsessive-compulsive behaviors in humans, these behaviors are hard to break and often treatment-resistant. OCD (Obsessive-Compulsive Disorder) in humans has been linked to reduced serotonin levels and dopamine sensitivity and are often the result of anxiety, stress and the sense of lack of control over one's environment.

Research shows that chronic stress in horses will increase beta endorphin levels. This rising beta endorphin level will result in dopaminergic super-sensitivity. This super sensitization of dopamine neurons in the brain will begin to lower the amount of stimulation necessary for the horse to develop stereotyped behaviors in any situation when they are aroused, excited or frustrated.

In other words, if endorphin levels are allowed to rise to the degree that compensatory behaviors like cribbing becomes pleasurable, the horse will resort to the stress-reducing behavior at the slightest level of arousal or agitation. However, these stereotypical patterns do not develop if the physiological arousal in the horse is not allowed to reach a critical limit.

Interestingly enough, favorable results have been seen in some cribbing horses released in the open among herd mates.

Several research studies have supported the positive impact pasture companionship has on learning. Research indicates that training takes far less time in pastured horses than stabled horses. Research also shows that confined horses, particularly racehorses and performance horses, exhibit much higher rates of behavioral problems.

CHAPTER SEVEN

Anthropomorphism

In the management of horses, we often use strategies to best satisfy human needs. Horses are movement and sensory animals with locomotion being an integral part of their makeup. They are sensory beings designed to seek comfort in numbers and to share in the responsibility of remaining alert for the herd's welfare. Their sensory systems are designed to scan the horizon and to provide protection by sensing threats at a distance. If a threat is detected, locomotion is their evolutionary, hardwired escape strategy. Therefore, they are most comfortable when they can put these ingrained functions to use.

However, we provide them with human housing. We put them in individual rooms with doors and roofs.

Horses are herbivores that require constant grazing and chewing to stimulate salivation. They need continual gut fill to maintain protection against gastric acidity. They need the bulk of forage to promote elimination.

But once again, we give them the human equivalent of breakfast, lunch and dinner with two to three "feedings" per day. If you don't think that feeding on a schedule produces agitation, arousal and stressful eating habits, then visit a farm when feeding time has been delayed.

Patting or slapping a horse on the neck is an ineffective reward and is often perceived as a punishment. Horses are not born with an innate understanding of patting.

Being sensory animals, horses have vibrissae, very sensitive "feelers" which have their own blood and nerve supply and are designed to protect vital areas (lips, eyes).

Horses are groomed according to human perceptions of beauty and therefore we decide they should be clean-shaven and have their whiskers lopped off. However, whiskers on humans are facial hair and vibrissae in horses are sensory organs.

Horses are dressed in human-made coats that inhibit their natural hair growth and inhibit the process by which their skin develops water resistance.

What do these management strategies have in common?

None are based on the horse.

The horses we have in America have been domesticated for hundreds if not thousands of years. We have been breeding them for several hundred generations. It's only been in the last half century that laws were passed in the U.S. restricting ranchers from managing horses on the open ranges of the West. So even though we have so-called wild horses or mustangs, those horses' gene pool has been in the hands of man for quite some time (up until the last 50 years). They're not like other North American wildlife.

We can use the characteristics of a so-called mustang in the wild that has had very little if any contact with man, and compare the characteristics of our domestic horses to recognize the impact we have on our horses.

We can look at horses confined and on rich diets and see problems with their neurological system, digestive system, skeletal system, and soundness issues. We do not see these problems in horses not confined and on the more moderate diet. We can learn that too much caring is not always the best care for the horse.

CONCLUSION

With this book, we have attempted to give information, based in science and observation, that readers can use to improve their horsemanship and horse management. We hope the anecdotes and neuroscience will allow readers to see horses in a clearer light. Ideally, readers will become improved horsemen and women, and their horses will be better off for it.

While *Evidence-based Horsemanship* might be a book with lots of facts, it's also an entirely new way of looking at things.

As you move forward with your horse, consider these EBH tenants:

1. The horse has survived and thrived for thousands of years in the natural setting. Any changes you introduce away from that natural setting will have an impact. You may not notice it, but varying levels of domestication will indeed impact the horse on a physiological and psychological level. If you use its original environment as a baseline and stick as close as possible to that baseline, your horse will be better off.

2. As you consider Evidence-Based Horsemanship and apply it to your horse training and management, you may want to experiment. As you do, it's important to understand the idea of **controls** and **variables**. If you

have multiple horses, you may try something new with one horse (shoes instead of bare hooves, stabling instead of pasture, grain instead of grass and hay), and leave the others unchanged. The trial horse will be the variable. The horses without any introduced change will be the controls. After some time, you will probably see differences between the two.

3. As you continue to gather information and learn, consider your sources. Stick to university studies, clinical studies, and other reports without bias and without any ulterior motives (like selling you something). As you consider these studies, keep in mind that the best research involves large numbers of horses. If you are looking at unscientific observation, consider those people who have observed thousands, not dozens of cases.

The weakest information is based on a single case or a single expert's opinion. Traditions, myths, or "just-the-way-we've-always-done-it" are similarly weak until tried with scientific method and proven to be effective and good for the horse.

GLOSSARY

Acetylcholine – all muscle movement is accomplished by the release of this neurotransmitter.

Adrenal cortex – the cortex of the adrenal gland; it secretes corticosterone and sex hormones.

Adrenal medulla – the medulla of the adrenal gland; it secretes epinephrine.

Adrenal pathway – (Hypothalamic/ Pituitary/Adrenal Pathway) the pathway involved when the amygdala responds to stress and activates the hypothalamus to chemically signal the adrenal glands to release glucocorticoid/cortisol into the bloodstream.

Adrenalin – A substance produced by the medulla (inside) of the adrenal gland; epinephrine. The secretion of adrenaline by the adrenal is part of the fight-or-flight response

Amygdala – almond shaped mass involved in emotional responses, hormonal secretions, and memory.

Analgesia – the absence of sensibility to pain or the relief of pain without loss of consciousness.

Anthropomorphism – attributing to animals those characteristics, motivations or behaviors that belong only to humans.

Autonomic Nervous System (self-governing) – control of basic vital functions such as regulation of smooth muscle, cardiac muscle, heart rate, blood pressure, breathing, body temperature, and digestion. The autonomic nervous system has sympathetic and parasympathetic divisions.

Axon – a long, slender projection of a nerve cell, or neuron, that conducts electrical impulses away from the neuron's cell body.

Basal ganglia – a group of nuclei that act as a cohesive functional unit. They are situated at the base of the forebrain and are strongly connected with the cerebral cortex, thalamus, and other brain areas.

Beta endorphin – naturally occurring opiate neurotransmitter released when the body is under stress; responsible for pain reduction.

Brainstem Reticular Activating System – a part of the reticular formation that extends from the brain stem to the midbrain and thalamus with connections distributed throughout the cerebral cortex and that controls the degree of activity of the central nervous system (as in maintaining sleep and wakefulness and in making transitions between the two states).

Caudate nucleus – a nucleus located within the basal ganglia, an important part of the brain's learning and memory system.

Cerebellum – a large structure that makes up approximately 1/3 of the horse's brain and coordinates movement. The cerebellum is continually making fine motor corrections to the horse's muscles that allow it to move smoothly, fluidly, and in a well -coordinated fashion.

Control – in an experiment, the control is something that remains unchanged. For instance, if you wanted to look at the impact of a new supplement, you might give Horse X the supplement and keep Horse Y's feed unchanged. Horse Y would be the control.

Cortex – the tissue forming the outer layer of an organ or structure.

Cortisol – stress-related steroid secreted by the adrenal cortex that helps the horse to make fats available for energy. It causes increases in blood flow and stimulates behavioral responses.

Cutaneous sensory information and adaptation – this information is provided by specialized receptors in the skin. These receptors provide information about vibration. The receptors will adapt to constant mechanical pressure unless the stimuli "flutter". Adaptation is when a moderate, constant stimulus applied to the skin fails to produce any sensation after it has been present for a while (e.g., the saddle or a rider's heavy leg).

Dendrites – branches that sprout from neurons containing neuroreceptors that capture chemical signals from neighboring neurons.

Dopamine – important neurotransmitter associated with reinforcement/reward and motor movement.

Endogenous – produced or grown from within.

Endogenous opioids – naturally produced chemicals that block pain and can produce sedation. The horse's brain possesses mechanisms that can reduce pain through endogenous opioids. Endogenous opioids will produce analgesia to reduce chronic, inescapable pain so that the horse can continue such vital behaviors as food finding, mating, and fighting. Pain tends to trigger escape and withdrawal responses. Subjectively, pain hurts and the horse tries hard to avoid it. However, sometimes the horse is better off ignoring pain and getting on with other tasks.

Endorphins – any of a group of endogenous peptides (as enkephalin and dynorphin) found in the brain that bind chiefly to opiate receptors and produce some of the same effects (as pain relief) as those of opiates.

Flocculonodular lobe – the posterior lobe of the cerebellum, concerned with equilibrium.

Forebrain – see frontal lobe.

Frontal lobe – or forebrain. An area in the front of the brain that is highly developed in humans and is associated with personality, future planning, and abstract thought. The greatest volume of white matter (myelination) in humans is in the frontal lobe. Horses have a more primitive frontal lobe involving mostly sensory or motor functions. The horse's frontal lobe is responsible for voluntary movement initiation and attention.

Functional MRI – Functional magnetic resonance imaging is a procedure that measures brain activity by detecting associated changes in blood flow.

Glial cells – Supportive cells in the central nervous system -- the brain and spinal cord. Glial cells do not conduct electrical impulses (as opposed to neurons, which do). The glial cells surround neurons and provide support for them and insulation between them.

Glucocorticoid – one of a group of hormones secreted by the adrenal system, especially in times of stress. Short-term effects of glucocorticoids are essential for the animal's well-being. Over the long-term, they are damaging to health, they raise blood pressure, damage muscle tissue, and can lead to steroid diabetes. They also suppress the immune system, making it more difficult to heal and making the animal vulnerable to infections. Gastric ulcers and enlarged adrenal glands are signs of chronic stress. Research with humans has shown that individuals with elevated blood levels of glucocorticoids learn more slowly.

Glutamate – an excitatory neurotransmitter.

Hebb Rule – Developed by Donald Olding Hebb, a Canadian psychologist, in 1949. When a cell is close enough to repeatedly excite an adjacent cell, a growth process or metabolic change takes place in both cells allowing for a more efficient information pathway that takes less powerful stimuli to excite in the future. It has thus been said: "neurons that fire together wire together."

Hypothalamus – a deep brain structure which sits below the thalamus and acts like a control system to regulate the autonomic nervous system and endocrine systems. The hypothalamus maintains status quo for a number of bodily functions, a process called "homeostasis".

Kinesthetic – relates to learning through feeling, such as a sense of body position, muscle movement, and weight as felt through nerve endings.

Medulla – the inner part of an organ or structure

Medullary pathway – the pathway through the brainstem that regulates breathing and controls sympathetic outflow to the heart and blood vessels.

Myelin – a fatty material that forms a layer, the myelin sheath, around the axon of a neuron. It is essential for the proper functioning of the nervous system.

Myelination – the process by which the fatty layer, myelin, accumulates around nerve cells (neurons). Myelination enables nerve cells to transmit information faster. The process is vitally important to healthy nervous system functioning.

Neostriatum – a compound structure comprised of the putamen and caudate nucleus.

Neuron – Any of the impulse-conducting cells that constitute the brain, spinal column, and nerves, consisting of a nucleated cell body with one or more dendrites and a single axon. Also called nerve cell.

Neuroreceptors – sites on dendrites which capture the chemical signal and convert it into an electrical signal and move the signal onward creating a chain of nerve signals.

Neurotransmitters – chemical compounds which act as messengers in the brain.

Olfaction – the sense of smell; the action or capacity of smelling.

Opiods – any of a group of natural substances, as the endorphins, produced by the body in increased amounts in response to stress and pain.

Parasympathetic Nervous System – part of the Autonomic Nervous System. It is involved with increasing the supply of stored energy (relaxation, restoration, increased blood supply to the gastrointestinal system). Parasympathetic motor nerves tend to be located around the horse's poll and hindquarters.

Physiology – the branch of biology dealing with the functions and activities of living organisms and their parts, including all physical and chemical processes.

Pituitary gland – part of the endocrine system, a small structure located just below the hypothalamus. It releases hormones that affect growth as well as influencing the activities of other glands.

Postsynaptic neuron – a neuron to the cell body or dendrite of which an electrical impulse is transmitted across a synaptic cleft by the release of a chemical neurotransmitter from the axon terminal of a presynaptic neuron.

Psychology – the study of mental processes and behavior.

Putamen – the part of the basal ganglion which comprises the external portion of the corpus striatum and which has connections to the caudate nucleus.

Relay nucleus – a nucleus of the brain that serves primarily to relay stimuli from lower receptor centers to coordinating cortical centers.

Reticular Activating System – a part of the reticular formation that extends from the brain stem to the midbrain and thalamus with connections distributed throughout the cerebral cortex and that controls the degree of activity of the central nervous system (as in maintaining sleep and wakefulness and in making transitions between the two states).

Reticular formation – A portion of the brain that is located in the central core of the brain stem. It passes through the medulla, pons, and stops in the midbrain. Its functions can be classified into four categories: motor control, sensory control, visceral control, and control of consciousness.

SAM system or axis (Sympathetic Adreno-Medullary System) – the SAM system influences body organs and parasympathetic responses to stress through the release of adrenaline.

Serotonin – a neurotransmitter that regulates mood.

Somatosensory Cortex – an area located in the mid part of the brain that processes input from various systems in the body that are sensitive to touch, including sensitivity to pain. This region also plays a role in providing information to the horse about where its body is situated in space (proprioception).

Somatic Senses – sensors in the skin that allow the horse to feel touch, pressure, pain, and temperature.

Stereotypies – frequent almost mechanical repetitions of the same posture or movement, with an irrelevant function.

Sympathetic Nervous System – part of the Autonomic Nervous System. It is involved in activities associated with expenditure of energy (fight or flight). Sympathetic motor nerves tend to be located in regions of the spinal cord.

Synapse – A junction between two nerve cells, consisting of a minute gap across which impulses pass by diffusion of a neurotransmitter.

Synaptic cleft – the space between neurons, measured in nanometers, at a nerve synapse across which a nerve impulse is transmitted by a neurotransmitter

Thalamus – an egg-shaped structure located in the center of the horse's brain. It is the hub for all incoming information with the exception of smell. The thalamus acts as a relay station, taking in signals and then relaying these messages that will ultimately activate muscles.

Trigeminal Nerve – the fifth cranial nerve. It has both motor and sensory components. It has three branches: the ophthalmic, the maxillary, and the mandibular. This nerve runs to the eye, the face, upper and lower jaw.

Variable – In an experiment, the thing that changes. For example, if you wanted to look at the impact of a new supplement, you might give Horse X the supplement and keep Horse Y's feed unchanged. Horse X would be the variable.

Vermis – the constricted median lobe of the cerebellum that connects the two lateral lobes.

Vestibular – Of or relating to a vestibule, particularly that of the inner ear, or more generally to the sense of balance.

Vestibular Nuclei – cells within the inner ear (vestibular nerve) that provide both postural information to the horse about the position of its head in relation to the rest of its body and a fixation point, so that a stable image remains on the retina as the head and body move.

Vomeronasal organ – an auxiliary olfactory sense organ; it contains sensory neurons that detect chemical stimuli. The vomeronasal organ is mainly used to detect pheromones, chemical messengers that carry information between individuals of the same species.

Acknowledgements

I owe a tremendous debt of gratitude to Maddy Butcher, owner of NickerNews.net, for her creative input and significant efforts in reading, organizing, and preparing the manuscript to make a much better book.

It would be impossible to list all those I consulted over the years in compiling data and writing *Evidence-Based Horsemanship*. I do wish to thank the numerous university-based veterinarian programs that graciously consulted with me in helping to verify our observations. I also wish to thank Jennifer Black, Kim Stone, Randy Rieman, Bryan Neubert, Steve Gabriel, Joyce Peters, and all the friends of Ray Hunt and Tom Dorrance. But mostly, I wish to acknowledge and thank the horses who are among the greatest teachers of all.

—Dr. Stephen Peters

Made in United States
Troutdale, OR
04/05/2024

18971525R00076